The Journey
to
Contentment

By Linda McBurney-Gunhouse

Published by:
Creative Focus Publishing
Winnipeg Beach, Manitoba
Canada

Cover photo & artwork by Linda McBurney-Gunhouse
ISBN: 978-1-928071-24-2
Copyright © 2012 Linda McBurney-Gunhouse
Reprinted 2025
All Rights Reserved.
R2.5

Published by:
Creative Focus Publishing
Box 704
Winnipeg Beach, Manitoba R0C 3G0 Canada
info@creativefocus.ca

Please visit our website:
www.creativefocus.ca

All Scripture is taken from the King James Version of the Bible unless otherwise stated.

Contents

Introduction

    This book has come about after a lifetime of searching for that sometimes hard-to-pin-down state of mind called contentment. Most people want to live a life of contentment, but they struggle to get there. Contentment can be very elusive, and it is something you can have today and lose tomorrow, or even within the next hour. But striving for contentment is worthwhile because being in a state of contentment is the most satisfying way to live life. With contentment comes joy and peace. When a person is content, they are truly living as, I believe, we are meant to live. Things may come and go, but a person who is content is not fazed by change. They can take it or leave it. Arriving at a state of contentment is paramount to living a happy and prosperous life, and yet the way to contentment can sometimes seem so hard because we want things to be different than they are right now. Some things we can change to bring about contentment and some things we can't change. When we fail to make the changes that are needed, we can become discouraged and feel like giving up. So we live our lives unhappy, and we may try to find joy and contentment in all the wrong places.

    Perhaps you are not happy with your current life circumstances, and things are not turning out for you the way you had imagined. You may find contentment temporarily, but it's a struggle to hold onto because something always comes along to disturb things, and then you find yourself discontent again. Perhaps you've had enough of living a frustrating and unfulfilled life, and you know that it's time for a change. This book will uncover what lies behind discontentment, why contentment can be so hard to arrive at, what is the ultimate source of it, and what life can be like once we get there. Come and enjoy the journey, and may God bless you as you travel towards that wonderful state of being we call "contentment."

Chapter 1
Beginning the Journey

Some people may not even realize it, but right now, they are working hard, striving to arrive at some sort of peaceful destination in their life. Most of us try many things, perhaps move around a lot, do some traveling, change jobs, or redecorate our home, but that place of peace and contentment eludes us. We may have had moments of complete satisfaction when everything seemed to come together, but it didn't take long for things to fall apart. Soon we find ourselves in a state of discontentment, and we have to start all over again on the path to finding contentment. Each time we find ourselves in a state of discontentment and try to find our way to contentment, we learn something new. So the first thing that is important to know about contentment is that it is often a process, and there is something to be learned with each step we take towards achieving it.

We often think that contentment has to do with setting goals and accomplishing them. When our goals are impeded or frustrated in any way, we can become discontent until those goals are reached. However, setting and reaching goals often provide only a brief and fleeting experience where we finally feel content. I remember the first time I felt not only a feeling of great accomplishment, but I experienced contentment as well. It was when I graduated from Grade 12. I had reached the goal of completing the first leg of my education, and now I could move on to the next step in life — going to college to learn a trade, and then getting a job and moving on in the world. But life threw me many surprises, and I made some foolish choices that thwarted my plans to be a successful journalist. My life took a completely different turn, and I had to abandon my life goals for being a journalist. I discovered that I had an anxiety disorder that would prevent me from working under the kind of strict deadlines and pressure that journalism demanded. Out of this disappointment because of my health, I struggled for many years to find contentment in a career. I did have typing and office skills that I had learned in high school, so this is the area I worked in right up until I got married. But I had wanted the excitement and adventure of always learning new things, and then writing about them, so working in an office was not at all interesting to me. For the most part, I suffered with discontentment.

As a Christian, with the feeling of discontent came guilt. I chided myself for feeling so out of sorts with my career and my life in general, since, according to the Bible, I was to learn to be content. I had read Paul's writings about it:

> *Not that I speak in respect of want: for I have learned, in whatsoever state I am, therewith to be content. Philippians 4:11*
>
> *I know both how to be abased, and I know how to abound: every where and in all things I am instructed both to be full and to be hungry, both to abound and to suffer need. Philippians 4:12*

So I tried to be content in my career as an office worker, but since my life goals of being a journalist were not forthcoming, and I couldn't find the adventure and excitement I was craving through research and writing, I had to find other ways to find fulfilment in my life. Sometimes, people in similar situations as mine turn to alcohol, drugs, gambling, or some other unhealthy vice. But, as with all vices, there are always negative consequences that only add to the problem. Fortunately for me, I did not turn to any of these vices. Instead, I just changed my focus from being a journalist to just simply being a writer. I loved reading and studying the Bible, so I wrote all kinds of articles based on certain topics that really interested me. For instance, I had a fascination with the idea of why a Christian backslides (turns away from God), largely because this is what had happened to me when I was a teenager. I wondered, *How can a Christian live in a sinful world, try to reach those that are unsaved, and not be affected by the slippery ways of the world?* Theologians call it "separation." I spent something like 20 years studying all about it until finally I had enough revelation and knowledge, as well as my own past experience, to write a book about it.

Something else I did while I worked in an unfulfilling job as an office worker was to ask God for more interests in my life. I knew I would always have the writing, but I wanted something more. So God granted me the desire of my heart. He began to show me that I was a history buff and that I also enjoyed nature and anything to do with the outdoors (including some sports). So I joined a historical society, and then I joined a naturalists club. I began to focus less on my unhappy career, and I shifted my thinking to history and nature. I attended all the meetings of my two new interests, went to every museum I could find, visited the naturalist's centers in the city and outside of the city, and I started to find a new purpose in life.

Some years went by, and I was relatively content, continuing to pursue my interests and adding new ones, like photography and art. I took courses, attended my church and got involved, made good friends at work, took little mini-vacations away from the city as often as possible, and found that I was living a satisfying and balanced life. But pretty soon another life goal came to the forefront. I was getting older, and I was still single; I really wanted to get married. Most of my friends were already married, and some of them even had children. I couldn't imagine not getting married, and even though this became an essential life goal for me, I would not just marry anyone. He had to be the right one, and he had to be God's choice for me. I was already seeing the break-up of some marriages, and I didn't want this to happen to me, so I prayed, and then I waited on God. I waited and waited, thinking that a friend I would be seeing might be the one, but these male friends came and went. Nearing the time I would finally know the right man I was to marry, I could think of nothing else but getting married.

During this time, God was preparing me and doing a deep work in my heart. Whenever God is doing a deep work in your heart, it is very often a difficult and painful process. And it seems that the longer you have to wait for something, the greater the result. Knowing how much I wanted to be married, God presented me with the ultimate test of loyalty to Him, and also the challenge to be content to remain single if He didn't provide a husband for me. Was I willing to remain single and still love Him and serve Him in that state? Then, He pointed out another desire of my heart that I already mentioned — to write full-time. Writing was all I had ever wanted to do, but so far, I had to put it aside and work in an office instead. I had hoped to marry someone who had a good paying job so he could support me in my writing aspirations. I wanted to quit my job working in an office. Now the Lord was asking me, *Would I be willing to continue working in an office to support my husband if need be?*

God is true to his Word. He was challenging me with the first commandment:

Thou shalt have no other gods before me. Exodus 20:3

Had I made the desire for a husband and the desire to write a god? Was I giving more attention to these requests than I was to the things of God? So now I wasn't sure what was going to happen. Like the Apostle Paul, I knew that I had to learn to arrive at a place of contentment with my life as a single, and I may have to continue working in an office indefinitely. But He also gave me hope not to give up completely my dream of being married and writing full time. Time and again He would remind of the following Scripture:

But seek ye first the kingdom of God, and his righteousness; and all these things shall be added unto you. Matthew 6:33

Contentment comes at a cost, and for a Bible-believing Christian, that cost means you have to make a concerted effort to dwell on the things of God above and beyond your own heart's desires. You have to be willing, at any time, to hand over your most intense wants and even needs and be willing to abandon them completely for the sake of the Kingdom. This is probably the most difficult test a Christian ever has to face in life.

After I was married, and I was able to write full-time (yes, I passed the tests that God presented me with), many years later, I found myself unhappy and discontent yet again. My husband and I were living in a resort town that was very quiet during the winter. I was writing, but I needed more stimulation, and I needed a change. My husband was away in the city working, and he had a long commute to work each day (3 hours in total), so we hardly even saw each other any more. We wanted a place in the city, closer to his work. Once again, God challenged me with, *Can you be happy here and trust Me with the way things are right now? Will you believe that this is My best for you in this moment?* I wondered how I could answer Him this time. After all, He had given me one of my greatest heart's desires — a loving Christian husband that I adored and who adored me; but we were separated by this long commute each day. I was in the country alone while he was in the city.

To add to the situation, by the time he got home, he was tired, and understandably, he needed lots of extra rest. Since I had been tested so many times before when it comes to the desires of my heart (I haven't mentioned other situations), I had learned to trust God, so I answered Him, Yes, I will be happy and content here alone without my husband if that is Your best for me right now. After I said this to God, unlike the situation when I wanted to be married and write full time, I was filled with a sense of peace and contentment. I looked around and really started to see how blessed I was. I had a wonderful home with windows everywhere; I was surrounded by the nature that I loved so much; I was married to an incredibly wonderful husband who supported me in my writing; I had a wonderful Christian family who loves me; I was healthy enough to enjoy my life, and I realized that things could always be a lot worse than they were at that moment. Not too long after that, God provided us with a spacious and beautiful townhouse in the city close to my husband's job, and we were still able to keep our house in the resort town. But the point is, I found contentment in the current state that I was in, even though I thought things could be a lot better than they were at the time.

Right now there are people who desperately want things. There are single people wanting a partner. They are married people wanting children but are unable to conceive or even adopt. There are unemployed people wanting a job, and there's people who are working in a job they don't really enjoy. There are people living in cramped apartments who would love to be able to buy a house. They are those that are sick that want to be healed so they can live a normal and healthy life. Everyone has needs and wants, and they can't understand why they feel so short-changed. Then there are others who seem to have everything they want in life, but they are still discontent.

Contentment is really a character-building process. God's ways are infinite and far superior to our ways. He uses our life circumstances, and the unmet desires of our hearts to test our commitment to Him and to grow us in the area of our faith. While we may rarely abandon our dreams, we must be willing to put them on the altar of sacrifice before God and let Him be first in our lives. The contentment that follows is so priceless, it can only be perceived as a great gift from God. Yet, sometimes, even though contentment is within our grasp, we live our lives in such a way that we prevent ourselves from ever experiencing it. Turn with me to the next chapter to look at what happens when we find ourselves driven to succeed, the cost involved, and how it affects our journey to contentment.

Chapter 2
Driven to Succeed

I mentioned earlier that one of the areas where I did a lot of studying was in the area of how a Christian can live in the world and still not become worldly (adopt sinful ways of the world and become ineffective as a Christian witness). I was truly surprised to discover that large portions of the Old Testament were about the often strained relationship the Children of Israel, God's chosen people, had with Him. It was often strained because the Children of Israel refused to walk in God's ways and serve Him with their whole heart, as they had been commanded to do. Yet God remained loving, forgiving, patient, and above all, faithful to His Word, in spite of their continued failure to obey Him. God had set up a covenant with them, that He would be their God and that they would be His people. This means they had to faithfully follow all of His ways, and love Him and serve Him unswervingly and sincerely from their heart. They were never to follow the ways of the world that surrounded them, since this would profoundly affect their relationship with God, and the covenant (based on their heart commitment to God) would fail on their part.

What was in it for the Children of Israel? Of all the people in the world, they were chosen by God to demonstrate who God is (see Deuteronomy 7:6). God would perform mighty miracles through them in such a way that the world would know the love, character, and mightiness of God. Why is this important? Because God loves the world in which He created, and it is His desire that each and every person come to know Him in a personal, meaningful, and life-changing way, but many of the children of Israel failed miserably. Instead of following God's ways, they turned away from Him and instead followed the pagan ways of the world around them. Time and again, God would discipline them, and they'd be captured and imprisoned by their pagan captors. They'd end up slaves to cruel masters, but still, God's love and kindness towards them never failed, and He'd free them from slavery and give them chance after chance.

Many people today are striving for something other than what God intends for them. They find themselves in a different kind of prison than one with physical bars. For one thing, our modern-day society is driven by the accumulation of money. Money means power, and people can use great wealth to manipulate and control other nations. But even on a smaller scale, we can get caught up in our market-driven society. We may be buying things we don't need and can't afford, and we pursue material things at an alarming rate. No wonder why personal debt is so high in so many households. We wonder why our credit card bills seem to soar and we have no savings. We can't seem to get ahead no matter how hard we try. We have to wonder where all this is taking us.

Major countries in the world are in deep financial debt. Somehow it got out of control and now, because of its tenuous financial status, has little bargaining power and has to sell off resources. When a nation becomes weakened, this is when other stronger nations can step in and start calling the shots. In short, you can lose your nation and all that it stands for. This is what happened to Israel. They were owned by their captors until God delivered them. They lost almost all of the land that was promised to them. This is what happens on a personal level in many households today. People are literally owned by the banks and lending institutions.

In my own case, I started to run a small business that involved purchasing supplies. It began as a greeting card photo business, and then it expanded over the years to include hand-made jewelry, sewing, artworks, and other crafts. I enjoyed the artistic life and making things, and I also enjoyed making a little bit of extra money. I also sold products for two different companies, which were expensive kitchen products and cosmetics for the other company. At one point, our 1,000+ square foot home was so packed full of stuff, I had to keep coming up with new and creative storage solutions so that the things I had purchased wouldn't completely take over our living space. I've regularly had to go through everything and get rid of a lot of it in order to have peace of mind and be able to live comfortably without having so much stuff. When you have too many things, it all takes time, either to look after, go through and give away, or discard altogether. So when we go shopping, rather than abandon ourselves to the idea of getting something new or different (even if it's something recycled), we must always consider the cost of time and space it will require. But even more than this, if it takes away from the things of God, then it must be abandoned altogether. For me, running the small business took away from the main goal of writing, which has been given to me as a way to spread the good news of the Gospel.

Like the children of Israel, Christians today can become just as ineffective and lose out on all that God desires for us, simply because we get too caught up in the race to succeed at almost any cost. Or we may get side-tracked, like I did when I kept expanding my photo card business. Years ago, I wrote an article called "No Compromise," and it was published in the local church bulletin. Several people commented on how much it had helped them. In the article, I talked about not so much how we get involved in the things of the world, but the fact that we've been called out of the world and that we are to no longer follow any of its ways. I quoted I Peter 2:9 and I'm adding verses 10 to 12 to further this discussion:

But ye are a chosen generation, a royal priesthood, an holy nation, a peculiar people; that ye should shew forth the praises of him who hath called you out of darkness into his marvellous light: (9)

Which in time past were not a people, but are now the people of God: which had not obtained mercy, but now have obtained mercy. (10)

Dearly beloved, I beseech you as strangers and pilgrims, abstain from fleshly lusts, which war against the soul; (11)

Having your conversation honest among the Gentiles: that, whereas they speak against you as evildoers, they may by your good works, which they shall behold, glorify God in the day of visitation. (12)

For a Christian, the only contentment to be found is in Jesus. It will never be found in the world. We must make a break with the world and all that it stands for. Yet, is this what we see happening today? While it is good to know what is happening, it is always unwise to try and fit in with the world, and in some cases, go to bed with it. You hear the word "relevance" in the local churches. Pastors and spiritual leaders wonder if their service is relevant to the outside world, and if they should change their worship service and style of service to attract unbelievers. In light of what the Bible has to say about it, I have serious misgivings when I hear of churches bending to the whims of the society around them in order to win the lost. Take a look at the following found in 2 Corinthians 6:14-18:

Be ye not unequally yoked together with unbelievers: for what fellowship hath righteousness with unrighteousness? and what communion hath light with darkness? (14)

And what concord hath Christ with Belial? or what part hath he that believeth with an infidel? (15)

And what agreement hath the temple of God with idols? for ye are the temple of the living God; as God hath said, I will dwell in them, and walk in them; and I will be their God, and they shall be my people. (16)

> *Wherefore come out from among them, and be ye*
> *separate, saith the Lord, and touch not the unclean*
> *thing; and I will receive you, (17)*

> *And will be a Father unto you, and ye shall be my sons*
> *and daughters, saith the Lord Almighty. (18)*

If we pay particular attention to verse 17, here in a nutshell, is the basis of the doctrine of separation. It's pretty clear, isn't it? We are to separate ourselves from the "ways" of the world, not the people in the world. Many people will argue that you can't win the lost unless you loosen up and lose the old-fashioned traditional ways. So we see some churches catering to the world and, in the process, becoming more and more like the outside world. Some churches provide mere entertainment and not the deep, holy, and meaningful things of God. It's interesting that when there's a crisis, however, people quickly discard entertainment, and they will seek those very same deep, meaningful, and life-changing things of God from days gone by. Many people are saved when they're in a crisis situation, especially if it is physically life-threatening.

One of the distinguishing characteristics of every Christian is contentment itself. After all, if we have been rescued from a life of sin and slavery to sin, how could we not be content in the new life in Christ we now abundantly enjoy? But if we go back to our former ways, we will blend in with the lost, and we will lose our testimony. There was a time many years ago when I tried to fit in with the world around me. I was single and reaching past 30. I really wanted to meet someone and one day get married. So I joined a non-Christian singles group. It was fun, as I went to dances and barbecues, parties and get-togethers, but as a Christian, I became lukewarm, to say the least. I did not stand out in the crowd, and I soon discovered just how shallow that party life really was. After awhile, my soul was tormented because I was not giving my all-in-all to the One who died for me, and paid for my life with His own precious blood. I had to quit the singles group. Maybe I was lonelier, but I was filled with a sense of peace and contentment, knowing I had done the right thing.

There are more verses that talk about separation from the world, found in Ephesians 5:6-13:

> *Let no man deceive you with vain words: for because of these things cometh the wrath of God upon the children of disobedience. (6)*
>
> *Be not ye therefore partakers with them. (7)*
>
> *For ye were sometimes darkness, but now are ye light in the Lord: walk as children of light: (8)*
>
> *(For the fruit of the Spirit is in all goodness and righteousness and truth;) (9)*
>
> *Proving what is acceptable unto the Lord. (10)*
>
> *And have no fellowship with the unfruitful works of darkness, but rather reprove them. (11)*
>
> *For it is a shame even to speak of those things which are done of them in secret. (12)*
>
> *But all things that are reproved are made manifest by the light: for whatsoever doth make manifest is light. (13)*

It takes boldness to stand out from the crowd and be separate, but there is great reward. As Christians, we will experience many highs and lows along life's pathway. But if we keep to the straight and narrow, and learn the ways of our Lord, we can say with Paul, "...**for I have learned, in whatsoever state I am, therewith to be content**" *(Philippians 4:11)*.

In the next chapter, we'll look further at another great hindrance to contentment, how people can embrace it, and what can happen when they do.

Chapter 3
Beware of Covetousness

Many years ago, I had an experience I will never forget. A friend came over and noticed all the stuff I had. Out of nowhere, and without being offensive, she kindly said that I had an issue with covetousness, and I should pray about it. So we prayed together, and after the prayer, something had changed, and I knew she was right. Up to that point, I had never really considered giving my things away or getting rid of them. I didn't know I was so attached to things, but after the prayer, I realized I had been holding onto things, and it served no purpose but to chain me to the things I had. Not long after that prayer, I started getting rid of things, mostly throwing them away, even though I found it difficult to part with them. These were things that I valued greatly, and things that had cost me. I realized later that it was something that I needed to do because, throughout my life, I have been able to more easily part with things and not form long attachments to them. Strangely enough, God has since blessed me with more things than I can even manage at times. Yet, since He knows I receive them and release them with an open hand and heart, He lets me enjoy things with few restrictions and for longer periods of time. Many times He replaces the things I give with something even better. I share this because covetousness has a lot to do with contentment. Going back to what Paul said,

> *I know both how to be abased, and I know how to abound: every where and in all things I am instructed both to be full and to be hungry, both to abound and to suffer need. Philippians 4:12*

When we experience both abundance and need, we become all the better for it. If we have little, we learn to appreciate having more, and when we have abundance, we can more easily give it up, since we will have already learned contentment, as Paul states in the previous verse:

> *Not that I speak in respect of want: for I have learned, in whatsoever state I am, therewith to be content. Philippians 4:11*

There is another passage of Scripture found in 1 Timothy 1:6 that offers an interesting truth about gain not being the way to contentment. If we look at the verses following verse 6, Paul also warns against covetousness. Here are the verses in 1 Timothy 1:6-11:

> *But godliness with contentment is great gain. (6)*
>
> *For we brought nothing into this world, and it is certain we can carry nothing out. (7)*
>
> *And having food and raiment let us be therewith content. (8)*
>
> *But they that will be rich fall into temptation and a snare, and into many foolish and hurtful lusts, which drown men in destruction and perdition. (9)*
>
> *For the love of money is the root of all evil: which while some coveted after, they have erred from the faith, and pierced themselves through with many sorrows. (10)*
>
> *But thou, O man of God, flee these things; and follow after righteousness, godliness, faith, love, patience, meekness. (11)*

It's not money that makes a person content, but godliness with contentment. At the time when I was learning about covetousness, I was also learning about money. I never made it a goal to be rich, but I saw money as a means to reaching my goals in life, as I think most people do. I had always wanted to travel, and that takes a lot of money. So somehow, the pursuit of money, in order to reach this lofty goal, took up far more of my thoughts than it should have. So the Lord began to teach me the truth about money and the pursuit of it. He directed me to Ecclesiastes 5:10-12:

> *He that loveth silver shall not be satisfied with silver; nor he that loveth abundance with increase: this is also vanity. (10)*
>
> *When goods increase, they are increased that eat them: and what good is there to the owners thereof, saving the beholding of them with their eyes? (11)*
>
> *The sleep of a labouring man is sweet, whether he eat little or much: but the abundance of the rich will not suffer him to sleep. (12)*

Solomon, who had great wealth, saw that there was a downside to having too much money. First, he recognized that money itself is not the answer, nor is accumulating more wealth and all the things it can buy. Most people who have wealth, or come upon sudden wealth, want everything money can buy, but this will never be enough. They will continue to want to buy more. Also, the more a person accumulates, the more he or she will have to worry about to the point that sleep will be hard to attain. I have known of some wealthy people who live in constant fear that they will be robbed or have their house broken into, so they buy an expensive security system. Some rich people can hire security personnel. Celebrities have to hide all the time to avoid people, cameras, and an adoring public. What kind of life is this?

Some wealthy people also wonder who they can trust, and if a friend wants them for friendship or for their money, so they restrict their social life to only other rich people. I have met wealthy people who were prejudiced towards others of a different social status, race, and color. I would find it difficult to make friends with some wealthy people because I have noticed a shallowness of character that I would struggle to be able to relate to. Then there are other wealthy people I know who have hoarded their money and would never want to part with any of it, even if they see others all around them with great needs. I have known of wealthy persons who have taken their own life because money and the pursuit of it was not enough for them, or because they had lost all their money that they had based their life on. But, I have also known and heard of wealthy people who have generously donated their wealth and made a difference in so many people's lives. I can think of two families that have done this out of all the wealthy people I have known. And I also know that some of the world's wealthiest people give generously to good causes, and others enjoy helping people in whatever way they can.

I have also known poorer people who worked hard for every dime they made, and then they freely, and without hesitation, gave generously with the little that they had. These have been some of the happiest people I have ever met. They had learned that contentment and happiness come from hard work and giving, rather than accumulating wealth and then hoarding it. For me, I have been somewhere in the middle, part of the average middle-class, always working and somehow being able to pay my bills, with some months more difficult than others. I feel most blessed to be in this position. The best place to be in, however, is not worrying about having too much money or about not having enough. To live a life striving for more money when a person really doesn't need more is unwise, and often a foolish waste of time.

There is a saying that God is in the moments of our lives. We may think big and plan big, but the really important and memorable parts of life all take place in the moment. If we are too busy accumulating wealth, we will miss out on these precious moments. Or conversely, if we are poor, we will be spending our time trying to find something to eat just to survive from one meal to the next. But the average person, who does honest work, will be able to pay his or her bills, enjoy their job, and enjoy their life after work and on weekends, and also enjoy a vacation once in awhile. We may not see this as a great gift of God, but according to Solomon, it is probably the best gift a person could possibly have as far as money and work go. Look at what he says in Ecclesiastes 5:18-20:

Behold that which I have seen: it is good and comely for one to eat and to drink, and to enjoy the good of all his labour that he taketh under the sun all the days of his life, which God giveth him: for it is his portion. (18)

Every man also to whom God hath given riches and wealth, and hath given him power to eat thereof, and to take his portion, and to rejoice in his labour; this is the gift of God. (19)

For he shall not much remember the days of his life; because God answereth him in the joy of his heart. (20)

In the New Testament, Jesus talks a lot about money. He also warns about covetousness, and then to illustrate the folly of it, He gives the famous parable of the rich man who had nothing better to do than to tear down his barns, and then build better ones to store his many goods. This is found in Luke 12:15-21:

And he said unto them, Take heed, and beware of covetousness: for a man's life consisteth not in the abundance of the things which he possesseth (15)

And he spake a parable unto them, saying, The ground of a certain rich man brought forth plentifully: (16)

And he thought within himself, saying, What shall I do, because I have no room where to bestow my fruits? (17)

And he said, This will I do: I will pull down my barns, and build greater; and there will I bestow all my fruits and my goods. (18)

And I will say to my soul, Soul, thou hast much goods laid up for many years; take thine ease, eat, drink, and be merry. (19)

> *But God said unto him, Thou fool, this night thy soul*
> *shall be required of thee: then whose shall those things*
> *be, which thou hast provided? (20)*

> *So is he that layeth up treasure for himself, and is not*
> *rich toward God. (21)*

Similar to what Solomon says, Jesus is wisely saying, *What good is it to have so much great wealth that you can't even enjoy it all, or you have no one to leave it to after you die?* If all we do is live to accumulate more wealth and bigger and better barns, and then we die, isn't this a waste of precious time and an unwise use of resources? How much does a person really need anyway? In one particular job I had when I was in my early 20s, older people were retiring after 35 or 40 years of working. Many of them died shortly after retiring. They never even got to enjoy the fruits of their labor after all the years of working. I often thought that perhaps they lived to work, rather than worked to live. So even in the case of making an honest living, without being able to enjoy the fruits of one's labour after retirement, could also be considered a form of striving after the wind that offers little reward, if any.

Jesus also talks about being anxious about having our needs met. When bills come in the mail, and we wonder how we're going to pay for things, there are two things we can always be assured of: God will always feed us, and He will always clothe us because He promised it in the following passage found in Luke 12:22-32.

> *And he said unto his disciples, Therefore I say unto you,*
> *Take no thought for your life, what ye shall eat; neither*
> *for the body, what ye shall put on. (22)*

> *The life is more than meat, and the body is more than*
> *raiment. (23)*

> *Consider the ravens: for they neither sow nor reap;*
> *which neither have storehouse nor barn; and God*

feedeth them: how much more are ye better than the fowls? (24)

And which of you with taking thought can add to his stature one cubit? (25)

If ye then be not able to do that thing which is least, why take ye thought for the rest? (26)

Consider the lilies how they grow: they toil not, they spin not; and yet I say unto you, that Solomon in all his glory was not arrayed like one of these. (27)

If then God so clothe the grass, which is to day in the field, and to morrow is cast into the oven; how much more will he clothe you, O ye of little faith? (28)

And seek not ye what ye shall eat, or what ye shall drink, neither be ye of doubtful mind. (29)

For all these things do the nations of the world seek after: and your Father knoweth that ye have need of these things. (30)

But rather seek ye the kingdom of God; and all these things shall be added unto you. (31)

Fear not, little flock; for it is your Father's good pleasure to give you the kingdom. (32)

Sell that ye have, and give alms; provide yourselves bags which wax not old, a treasure in the heavens that faileth not, where no thief approacheth, neither moth corrupteth. (33)

For where your treasure is, there will your heart be also. (34)

In the last verse, Jesus proclaims a bold truth: *For where your treasure is, there will your heart be also.* Remember further up in Luke, Jesus warns against covetousness and that a person's life is much more than owning things. Yet how often do we pay more attention to the things we own than we do to the things of God? What are the important things that matter to God? It's people, of course, the same people He created, loves, and gave His life for. If people are what is most important to God, then things, and coveting them, can never take a place in our hearts. We must always receive with an open hand and also be willing to relinquish whatever God has allowed us to enjoy. This way, our hearts will remain untouched by the desire for all the things this world has to offer. Rather than anxiety about how much we have to gain or lose, we will be granted that most wonderful gift of contentment instead.

In the next chapter, we'll look at how contentment sometimes comes at a cost, and what can stand in the way of achieving contentment if we are not aware of what can be sabotaging our goal to get there.

Chapter 4
The Cost of Contentment

It takes great courage to follow your convictions and stand up for what you believe. Even if everyone else around you is doing the same thing and you do something different, it is better to live according to your convictions, than to follow the crowd and live a life of dis-ease and discontentment. Sometimes the greatest impediment to achieving contentment is when we are too easily swayed by what others think of our goals and decisions. So many times I have heard of a person who wants to pursue a certain career, but a parent or someone else will talk them out of it. So that person will never really find fulfillment and will have difficulty achieving contentment if they never pursue what they really want to do in life.

But then I also know of people who went against the grain and did pursue what they loved to do. My father was one of those people, and I always admired him for choosing his sales career when he could have had his pick of government jobs. He was a happy person as a result of it. Many times, rather than come home unhappy and depressed from working at a job he truly disliked, he would come home as happy as when he had left for work, sometimes happier. He would tell us all about his travels, the people he met, the things he saw, and what he had sold that day. Many times he would bring some small thing for us kids that he would have bought, like chips, gum, or chocolate bars. I can't help but think that he had an influence on me when later in life I too started selling things, and eventually I abandoned my government office job to pursue a writing career, and also pursue my artistic interests. Yet, in spite of many people having to work at jobs they really dislike, contentment is possible regardless, even though it will take more of an effort to achieve it.

In addition to not pursuing a career of choice because of the advice of well-meaning parents or other people, there are many other areas where people will come along and unwittingly impede our goals to contentment. Sometimes people will determine our whole lifestyle if we let them! What happens is that we may want to please our family and friends and not risk rejection or hurting their feelings, so we agree to everything they want us to do. Our own plans, hopes, and dreams get laid aside because we never say "no" to others when, really, we should be far more discriminating when it comes to agreeing to do things. For instance, if you have a friend that likes to organize and manage events, they will expect you to go along with whatever it is they are planning. It may be a party, a movie night, or any other kind of social gathering, which isn't convenient for you, but you will go anyway. And if you keep allowing this friend to dictate to you this way, you will not find peace or contentment until you start saying no to their wants and needs. Sometimes we settle for friends that are demanding, even though it costs us a great deal, not realizing that there are other friends available who would never put so many demands on us.

The ideal friend is someone who shares similar interests to you, most often agrees with your own style of doing things, and shares the same vision, passion, and purpose that you have. The Apostle Paul had his priorities straight. He was called to preach the Gospel and also minister to the churches. He had to be very discerning when it came to his team of helpers. In 1 Timothy 4:10-22, we find out who the workers are, who is effective to him in the ministry, and who is not.

For Demas hath forsaken me, having loved this present world, and is departed unto Thessalonica; Crescens to Galatia, Titus unto Dalmatia. (10)

Only Luke is with me. Take Mark, and bring him with thee: for he is profitable to me for the ministry. (11)

And Tychicus have I sent to Ephesus. (12)

The cloke that I left at Troas with Carpus, when thou comest, bring with thee, and the books, but especially the parchments. (13)

Alexander the coppersmith did me much evil: the Lord reward him according to his works: (14)

Of whom be thou ware also; for he hath greatly withstood our words. (15)

At my first answer no man stood with me, but all men forsook me: I pray God that it may not be laid to their charge. (16)

Notwithstanding the Lord stood with me, and strengthened me; that by me the preaching might be fully known, and that all the Gentiles might hear: and I was delivered out of the mouth of the lion. (17)

And the Lord shall deliver me from every evil work, and will preserve me unto his heavenly kingdom: to whom be glory for ever and ever. Amen. (18)

Salute Prisca and Aquila, and the household of Onesiphorus. (19)

Erastus abode at Corinth: but Trophimus have I left at Miletum sick. (20)

Do thy diligence to come before winter. Eubulus greeteth thee, and Pudens, and Linus, and Claudia, and all the brethren. (21)

The Lord Jesus Christ be with thy spirit. Grace be with you. Amen. (22)

Starting in verse 10, Paul recounts the people who have been ministering with him and gives an account of their usefulness or lack of support. Then sadly, when we get to verse 16, Paul mentions that everyone but the Lord forsook him. Also, we can see in verse 17 that Paul had a single-minded goal to ensure the Gospel was preached, and especially that it would reach the Gentiles. Paul would let nothing or no one stand in his way, as we see in verse 14, where he talks about Alexander, who did him much evil, and then in the next verse, he gives a warning because Alexander has caused a great deal of trouble. What I notice in this particular passage of Scripture is that Paul doesn't hesitate to give praise where it's due, and he gives rebuke and warning when it's needed. He is not trying to please his team of ministry helpers, but he's only striving to please the Lord. As we read more of the writings of Paul, it becomes clear that Paul was very close to the Lord and walked with Him, thereby enabling him to be able to discern the people who would support him, and those who would be a hindrance to him. Clearly, the cost of contentment comes at the price of cutting loose the people in our lives who serve as a hindrance, and prevent us from doing and being all that we're meant to be.

While other people may create a hindrance to us in achieving peace and contentment, many times it is our own selves that stand in the way. We may have a vision and a goal, but we are too afraid to take a chance and start pursuing our dreams and passions in a determined way. Our goals may seem so out of reach we don't even know how or where to begin, so we settle for the safe and comfortable. In my case, as I mentioned before, I wanted to write full-time and not work in an office for the rest of my life. Even though it ended up happening in God's perfect timing, I still worked towards that goal behind the scenes of God's miraculous workings. Just because we pray and believe that God will grant the desire of our heart, it doesn't always mean that we sit back and do nothing. In some cases, we also have to use the skills, the brain, and the brawn that God gave us. He expects us to work towards our goals while at the same time trusting Him to bring the things to pass that we have no control over, or can't obtain ourselves. Real faith means that if we really believe in our goals and dreams, and that they are God-given, then it only makes sense that we do everything we can to reach these goals. There is a very important aspect in our Christian life if we are to grow in our faith, and that is to put action to our hopes and dreams. Without action, our words and desires are empty, and we will not get very far. Look at what it says in James 2:20-24:

> *But wilt thou know, O vain man, that faith without works is dead? (20)*
>
> *Was not Abraham our father justified by works, when he had offered Isaac his son upon the altar? (21)*
>
> *Seest thou how faith wrought with his works, and by works was faith made perfect? (22)*
>
> *And the scripture was fulfilled which saith, Abraham believed God, and it was imputed unto him for righteousness: and he was called the Friend of God. (23)*
>
> *Ye see then how that by works a man is justified, and not by faith only. (24)*

If faith without works is dead, as it says in verse 20, then it is imperative that we get to work, and believe that one day we will reach our goals and live out our dream.

In my case, I began to move towards my goals by enrolling in university. Before ever enrolling, however, I mentally prepared myself to read more studious-type books, and long books of classic literature cover to cover, just to make sure I could read through and understand university-level books. I had done lots of reading but had never voluntarily read these types of books. I wanted to major in English and take my minor in Political Studies, so those were the types of books I read cover to cover. Surprisingly, I enjoyed them so much that I read everything I could get my hands on. Then I knew I was prepared for the discipline of university. After six long years of taking night school and summer school while working full time at my job, I finally finished and graduated with a Bachelor of Arts degree. What a tremendous feeling of accomplishment. I had given up huge chunks of my life and five full summers to do it, and I had researched and written dozens of essays. I had learned so much that I thought I would burst. The world had been opened up to me in a new way, and I now understood things so much clearer that I wondered how I had ever gotten through life not knowing even how the political system was run and why. I understood things from a historical perspective; I had learned something about science and weather patterns, religious history and political ideologies, psychology, and sociology. I was fascinated by what I had learned, and all because I had believed in my dreams and that I could accomplish this goal.

Yet still, I knew there was more that I had to do in order to reach my ultimate goal of writing full-time. Contentment in reaching this goal was still a ways off, so there was more that I had to do. When I had first chosen my courses for the BA, I had deliberately picked courses that would count towards another after-graduate degree in Education. I would only need to go to school for two more full years, and I would have a Bachelor of Education degree and then be able to teach. If I became a teacher, I would have summers off, be able to buy a cottage, and spend the summers at the lake writing. It was the only career I could think of that would pay well enough and give me the time off to be able to write. Three years after I graduated from university with my BA, surprisingly, I got married, another wonderful answer to prayer that God completely orchestrated. I quit my government job and began writing full time.

Three years after we were married, it was time to complete the next leg of my goal, and that was to return to university and complete my education. Even though I was able to write full-time, the skills I would receive from the Bachelor of Education were invaluable in adding to my writing and organizing abilities, and also it would give me an opportunity to one day teach what I was writing. After graduating two years later with honors, I began teaching ESL, since I had also received certification in that area. From taking the degree in Education, my writing greatly expanded, and I began writing family histories as well as topical books based on Biblical doctrines and Scriptures. One of the family histories I completed was my mother's family. In this lengthy book, I received almost 20 testimonies from my aunts and uncles and how they each miraculously became saved after leaving a Catholic church that did not teach the salvation message. My writing career turned into publishing and grew from there. I have written well over 20 books[1] and continue to publish them.

For me, I had to do everything I could possibly do, at a great personal cost, in order to reach the goals, passions, and desires of my heart. The contentment I enjoy today in being able to do what I believe I was always meant to do is, without a doubt, a great gift from God. But it was never easy. Many times I wanted to quit and give up my studies. Sometimes my writing was far more difficult than I imagined. For instance, one of my books, *Victory Over Backsliding*, took me over 20 years of research, and I wrote it five times before I came up with the final copy to publish. Writing takes discipline, and many times I have found myself alone with my thoughts when I would have rather gone on a social outing, but this is the goal I have worked so hard to achieve. I know that there is nothing better for me except to keep writing, and to do so with all my heart, strength, and determination.

Perhaps you have a goal and a dream and a vision for your life, but you have not yet taken a step on your journey to fulfillment and contentment in the areas you feel most drawn to. Maybe others have discouraged you or kept you so busy and distracted that you haven't even thought about taking a bold risk and making a change in your life. Remember, for everything worthwhile that will bring untold joy

---

[1] I now have over 50 books written and published (as of 2025); see "Other Titles" at the back of this book.

and contentment in your life, there is a price to pay. It is up to each and every one of us to decide if we are willing to pay that price.

In the final chapter, we'll discover what it's like to live a life of contentment, and why it's so important that we strive to get there and continue to stay there.

Chapter 5
The Place of Contentment

On a spiritual level, and in every other area of our life, the ultimate source of our contentment is Jesus. If we never reach all of our goals and dreams in this life, and all we have is Jesus, then we have all that we will ever need, and so much more than we could ever imagine. If you have ever experienced Jesus in a personal way, then you would agree without hesitation that when you've spent time with Him, nothing in this world or in this life can compare to that wonderful experience. Jesus is pure love, and He fills our every longing just by His presence. The contentment that comes with knowing Him makes us satisfied and complete. Nothing can compare to Jesus; everything else in life is temporary and will never complete us because we'll always want something more. When we find Jesus and accept Him into our life, we have reached that place of contentment and fulfillment. Everything we have been living for up until that point will seem worthless to us. Jesus said it so well in Matthew 13:44-46:

> *Again, the kingdom of heaven is like unto treasure hid in a field; the which when a man hath found, he hideth, and for joy thereof goeth and selleth all that he hath, and buyeth that field. (44)*
>
> *Again, the kingdom of heaven is like unto a merchant man, seeking goodly pearls: (45)*
>
> *Who, when he had found one pearl of great price, went and sold all that he had, and bought it. (46)*

Just think of the great worth of finding a treasure so great you would give all that you had for it. This is the joy of the discovery of the great worth of the things of God that are so much greater than the temporary things of this world. And in the following verses found in Hebrews 13, we have something very similar:

> *Let your conversation be without covetousness; and be content with such things as ye have: for he hath said, I will never leave thee, nor forsake thee. (5)*

> *So that we may boldly say, The Lord is my helper, and I will not fear what man shall do unto me. (6)*

In the NIV version of the Bible, verse 5 reads:

> *Keep your lives free from the love of money and be content with what you have, because God has said, "Never will I leave you; never will I forsake you." Hebrews 13:5*

When I first read this verse (5), I meditated on it and thought about what it meant. I realized that it means when you know Jesus in a personal way, you have everything you will ever need. He provides all our needs, but even more, He never leaves us, and no matter what, He never forsakes us. What more could we ask for?

Even though I was raised in a Christian home, I turned away from God when I was just a teenager. I was restless and curious about experiencing the things of the world, outside of the bounds of what the Bible said about it. I wanted to explore all that the world had to offer. I didn't realize that any path you take in life without Jesus as your Guide and His Word as your source of comfort and direction, is a cleverly disguised path of darkness that ultimately leads to destruction. Jesus warns us about this in Matthew 7:

> *Enter ye in at the strait gate: for wide is the gate, and broad is the way, that leadeth to destruction, and many there be which go in thereat: (13)*

> *Because strait is the gate, and narrow is the way, which leadeth unto life, and few there be that find it. (14)*

I discovered much later on that when the Bible tells you something, it IS TRUE, and it will come to pass just as it says it will. People may argue that the Bible is just a book of myths, and they don't believe any of it, but it doesn't change the truth of what it says. God cannot lie, and when He speaks His Word, whatever He declares will happen, regardless of whether or not a person believes it will. A person has only to continue to reject God to find out too late that they are lost in their sin, and they will never make it into heaven after they physically die unless they have already accepted the salvation He freely offers.

People have said that there are many roads that lead to God, but truthfully, there is only one.

Jesus saith unto him, I am the way, the truth, and the life: no man cometh unto the Father, but by me. John 14:6

I found out that there is an abrupt end to the pleasures of sin (see Hebrews 11:25), and there is a destructive end when you follow the ways of the world.

There is a way which seemeth right unto a man, but the end thereof are the ways of death. Proverbs 14:12

I ended up incapacitated and suffering with a nervous breakdown from the ungodly and destructive life I had been living. When I attended Bible School during this time since there was literally no place else to go, in spite of my resistance to the things of God, I became fascinated with the study of salvation (soteriology) and the state of sin and how it affects a person. The book of Romans became my favourite book of the Bible since Paul goes into great detail to explain it all. I had always thought that a person chooses to sin and that there are both good and bad people. This is a very common misperception, and one that will cost many people eternal life in heaven. They will die without hope because only Jesus can save us by His perfect work of atonement He provided for us when He died on the cross. According to Romans, **everyone sins**, and God does not measure a person's worth by whether they are good or bad. It says there are none that do good, no, not even one person, as the following verse testifies.

> *They are all gone out of the way, they are together become unprofitable; there is none that doeth good, no, not one. Romans 3:12*

Sin is a state that we are all born into, and we each have a sin nature that compels us to sin. In fact, in Romans 6:6, it says we "serve" sin:

> *Knowing this, that our old man is crucified with him, that the body of sin might be destroyed, that henceforth we should not serve sin.*

In Romans 6:12-20, Paul says we "obey" sin. Again in verses 17 and 20, he says we are "servants" to sin. Also in this text, Paul explains that only when we come to Christ are we freed from being servants to sin.

> *Let not sin therefore reign in your mortal body, that ye should obey it in the lusts thereof. (12)*
>
> *Neither yield ye your members as instruments of unrighteousness unto sin: but yield yourselves unto God, as those that are alive from the dead, and your members as instruments of righteousness unto God. (13)*
>
> *For sin shall not have dominion over you: for ye are not under the law, but under grace. (14)*
>
> *What then? shall we sin, because we are not under the law, but under grace? God forbid. (15)*
>
> *Know ye not, that to whom ye yield yourselves servants to obey, his servants ye are to whom ye obey; whether of sin unto death, or of obedience unto righteousness? (16)*

But God be thanked, that ye were the servants of sin, but ye have obeyed from the heart that form of doctrine which was delivered you. (17)

Being then made free from sin, ye became the servants of righteousness. (18)

I speak after the manner of men because of the infirmity of your flesh: for as ye have yielded your members servants to uncleanness and to iniquity unto iniquity; even so now yield your members servants to righteousness unto holiness. (19)

For when ye were the servants of sin, ye were free from righteousness. (20)

Also, in the NIV version of the Bible, we find in Romans 7:14 that we are "slaves" to sin.

We know that the law is spiritual; but I am unspiritual, sold as a slave to sin.

Therefore, to say that we are good (meaning that we don't choose to sin) means nothing at all, since good behavior can never release us from the grip and effects of sin (which is death) that we are all born with. When I discovered that I was sinning because I was born with a sin nature, and not because I was a "bad" person, I rejoiced in the hope that God would accept me, not because of my behavior, but because of His Son, Jesus Christ, who forgave me when He died on the cross, and accepted me as His beloved child when I received Him into my life.

In addition to this, Jesus gives us new life and removes the devastating effects of sin, which are death and eternal separation from Him.

Therefore if any man be in Christ, he is a new creature: old things are passed away; behold, all things are become new. 2 Corinthians 5:17

I remember when the truth of this verse started to take effect for me. I could hardly believe what was happening! The things that I was holding onto, from drugs to rock and roll music, melted away, and I no longer had the compulsion to turn to these things as a way to get me through the day. I didn't feel the heavy weight of sin in my heart like I did before. I didn't feel the guilt of living a sinful life. I felt light-hearted and free for the first time ever. Many other things changed for me, as well. I now had a best Friend in Jesus, and I didn't feel so alone. I made new friends who really knew how to have fun without having to get drunk or stoned on drugs. I laughed heartily without the demonic influence of drugs, and I went to bed at night with peace in my heart. I had a new purpose, and I was excited about my life and what I would do to serve Jesus, who had died for me and loved me with His very life! I had never known such love before. How could He forgive me, and then accept me as His own beloved child, after all I had done that went against everything He stood for?

When we receive Jesus, we are no longer slaves to sin. I knew, when I came to a point of desperation when I was so depressed I could hardly get out of bed, that there was nothing I could do to rise from the deep pit of despair I was in. Many people, in a similar desperate situation, will start to bargain with God. They say, "I promise I'll change, and I'll never do these bad things again," yet, because of our inborn sin nature, it is futile to make such a promise. We may stop one bad bahavior by sheer willpower, but it still does not stop us from sinning in other areas. Sin will always be acted out as a result of our sinful state of being. Even our thoughts are sinful, and we may not even realize it. This is where people are so confused! They think that they can deliver themselves from their own sin by their good works, and at the end of their life, they think that because they never killed someone or stole anything, that this is good enough for God! But God's standards are so much higher. We would have to be 100% sinlessly perfect from the day we are born until the day we die, and this is just not possible. Who would dare think that they are sinlessly perfect? And who are we to judge what is good in the first place?

My testimony to the greatness and love of God is that he freed me from the compulsion to sin, and I no longer had the desire to sin like I had before. He removed the power that sin had over me. I am an overcomer! Only God can perform such a miraculous act. What results from this is peace with God, and with that, comes ultimate contentment. Without being at peace with God, we live with a constant fear of what happens to us after we die. We have no assurance of our ultimate destination after we pass from this life.

Perhaps you are reading this right now, and you are not quite sure that your heart is right with God and that He will accept you into His heaven after you die. Perhaps you have never had contentment in your life, but you've gone from one thing to the next, never to find the peace, joy, and happiness that you seek. Today can be the start of a new day for you. If you'd like to take the most important step you can ever take towards the life you have been searching for and have not yet found, please turn to "The Way of Salvation" located in the next section. In Jesus, you will be in the place of contentment, and He will be with you all throughout your journey through this life.

The Way of Salvation

In all of life, no one loves you more than God does. He loved you so much He sent His own Son to die on a cross, then He raised Him up again, and He lives forevermore. When Jesus died, a phenomenal thing happened — He willingly took all our sins and sicknesses upon Himself so that we wouldn't have to bear them ourselves. He forgave us the huge debt of sin we owed to God, so that we could be pardoned and set free to live a life unto Him. Salvation is free and open to all who call upon the name of the only One who can truly save us. If you haven't already taken this important step, you are invited to accept Jesus into your heart and life today. Begin by reading the following Scriptures to begin your new life, and don't delay!

Today is the day of salvation ...

> *(For he saith, I have heard thee in a time accepted, and in the day of salvation have I succoured thee: behold, now is the accepted time; behold, now is the day of salvation.) 2 Corinthians 6:2*

We are all in need of salvation ...

> *For all have sinned, and come short of the glory of God; Romans 3:23*

Good works cannot save you ...

> *They are all gone out of the way, they are together become unprofitable; there is none that doeth good, no, not one. Romans 3:12*

> *Not by works of righteousness which we have done, but according to his mercy he saved us, by the washing of regeneration, and renewing of the Holy Ghost; Titus 3:5*

The Lord will never turn away anyone who truly wants to know Him ...

> *For whosoever shall call upon the name of the Lord shall be saved. Romans 10:13*

Jesus is the only One who can save us ...

> *Neither is there salvation in any other: for there is none other name under heaven given among men, whereby we must be saved. Acts 4:12*

> *That at the name of Jesus every knee should bow, of things in heaven, and things in earth, and things under the earth; Philippians 2:10*

Salvation gives us eternal life with Jesus ...

> *For God so loved the world, that he gave his only begotten Son, that whosoever believeth in him should not perish, but have everlasting life. John 3:16*

> *For God sent not his Son into the world to condemn the world; but that the world through him might be saved. John 3:17*

But every person is condemned without Jesus ...

> *He that believeth on him is not condemned: but he that believeth not is condemned already, because he hath not believed in the name of the only begotten Son of God. John 3:18*

We have an assurance of salvation ...

> *And I give unto them eternal life; and they shall never perish, neither shall any man pluck them out of my hand. John 10:28*

> *My Father, which gave them me, is greater than all; and no man is able to pluck them out of my Father's hand. John 10:29*

Dear Friend,

If you would like to receive Jesus into your heart and life today and also have the assurance that you will spend eternity in heaven with Him, please begin by saying this prayer:

Dear Heavenly Father,

I come to you in the name of Jesus. Your Word says, "Whosoever shall call upon the name of the Lord shall be saved" (Acts 2:21). I call on you now, and ask Jesus to come into my heart, forgive me for all my sins, and cleanse me. I ask you to be Lord over my life, according to Romans 10:9-10 — "That if thou shalt confess with thy mouth the Lord Jesus, and shalt believe in thine heart that God hath raised him from the dead, thou shalt be saved. For with the heart man believeth unto righteousness; and with the mouth confession is made unto salvation." I do this now — I confess that Jesus is Lord, and I believe in my heart that God raised Him from the dead.

In Jesus Name,
Amen

You are now reborn! You are a Christian and a child of God! Be assured, you have taken the most important step of your life, and God has reserved your place in heaven. He will always be with you, and lead you into all truth:

But the Comforter, which is the Holy Ghost, whom the Father will send in my name, he shall teach you all things, and bring all things to your remembrance, whatsoever I have said unto you. John 14:26

...for he hath said, I will never leave thee, nor forsake thee. Hebrews 13:5b

You will need to read the Bible on a daily basis to get to know Him, and all the many promises He has for you. As well, don't delay in contacting a Bible-believing church, where you will find fellowship with others who have also taken this important life-changing step. May God bless you as you continue on your new path of life, and freedom in Christ!

About the Author

Linda McBurney-Gunhouse enjoys her life in Manitoba, Canada. She writes to help others and inspire them to overcome difficulties and achieve success in life. She also enjoys story-telling in the form of writing fiction. Linda has spent a life-time writing and honing her skills. She studied Journalism, English, and History and received both a BA and B.Ed. in English. She has a diploma in magazine writing. She has worked as a contributing editor for a community college newspaper, and also as an editor for a community newspaper in Winnipeg. Her articles have appeared in national, city, and community newspapers and one magazine. She has written and sold one radio play. She is an accomplished eBook author of several inspirational books, including five full-length fiction. Her readership is international, and some of her eBooks frequently reach the Top 100 in specific categories. Linda also writes thought-provoking blogs.

Linda loves to share her faith and how she has overcome the many challenges in life in a way that readers can relate to. She sometimes teaches Creative Writing, and she does special speaking. Occasionally, she does free-lance writing for the local newspapers. She has also facilitated her own online and in-person writers' group. She continues to expand her thought-provoking blogs and book-writing. When she is not writing, she loves to be involved in creating art.

Other Titles

By Linda McBurney-Gunhouse

Inspirational Books

Cures for Stress
Essential Steps to Increase Your Faith
Footpath to Freedom
Freedom Through Spiritual Discernment
Healing & Hope for Child Loss
Healing For The Wounded Soul
Loneliness: The Pathway to Discovery
Making Sense of the Rapture
Money: Master or Servant?
No Fear of Hell
Power Thoughts for Positive Thinking
Spiritual Leadership in a Fallen World
The Act of Decision-Making
The Bible: Conformed or Transformed?
The Journey of Oneness
The Journey to Contentment
The Power of Submission
Victory Over Backsliding
When Love Is All There Is

Biography

The Bonk Saga: A History of Memories
Called to Overcome

Devotionals

Pathways to Devotion I
Pathways to Devotion II
Pathways to Devotion III
Pathways to Devotion IV
Pathways to Devotion V
Pathways to Devotion VI
Pathways to Devotion VII
Pathways to Devotion VIII
Pathways to Devotion IX
Pathways to Devotion X
Pathways to Devotion XI
Pathways to Devotion XII

Fiction

The Redemption of Steep Rock Cove
Return to Steep Rock Cove
Christmas Comes to Steep Rock Cove
Waves of Change at Steep Rock Cove
Driving with the Top Down
Track Three
Joanna's Secret Treasure

Poetry Books

Heart Songs
Songs in the Desert
Water Crossings
Wings I: Morning Arising
Wings II: Daylight Reflections
Wings III: Contemplation
Wings: Inspirational Poetry Series

Creative How-to Books

Artistic Ideas & Inspirations
How to Create Stories From Your Own Life
Living a Creative Life

Writing Manuals

Creative Writing
Write Your Life Story
Fiction Writing

Please visit our website at www.creativefocus.ca to discover the many books from this list that are available as eBooks.

Note: If you have enjoyed reading this book, or any other eBook of mine, please rate it online, or recommend it on your Facebook page. It will help spread the word, and let others know it is available. My goal is to help, encourage and inspire others through my writing. Thank you and may God richly bless you!

www.ingramcontent.com/pod-product-compliance
Lightning Source LLC
Chambersburg PA
CBHW070038070426
42449CB00012BA/3088